you are

Adi Welp

you are

Advantage BOOKS

a journal of His voice

adi welp

You Are: A Journal of His Voice by Adi Welp
Copyright © 2023 by Adalyn Welp
All Rights Reserved.
ISBN: 978-1-59755-779-5

Published by: ADVANTAGE BOOKS™, Longwood, FL
                  www.advbookstore.com

All rights reserved. No portion of this book may be reproduced, stored in a retrieval system, or transmitted in any form or by any means—electronic, photocopy, recording, scanning, or other—except for brief quotations in critical reviews or articles, without the prior written permission of the publisher.

Bible quotations are taken from the New Living Translation version of the Bible. Copyright 2008-2023 by Life.Church Bible app.

Library of Congress Catalog Number: 2023947889

Name: Welp, Adalyn, Author
Title: You Are: A Journal of His Voice
                  Adi Welp
                  Advantage Books, 2023
Identifiers: ISBN Paperback: 978159757795, eBook: 978159757962
Subjects: RELIGION: Christian Life – Inspirational

First Printing May 2024
23 24 25 26 27 28   10 9 8 7 6 5 4 3 2 1

You Are: A Journal of His Voice

Table of Contents

YOU ARE MADE NEW 8

YOU ARE RESCUED 10

YOU ARE MADE IN THE IMAGE OF GOD 12

YOU ARE FOUGHT FOR 14

YOU ARE CARED FOR 16

YOU ARE NOT ALONE 18

YOU ARE IN HIS VISION 20

YOU ARE HEARD 22

YOU ARE CLEANSED 24

YOU ARE FILLED 26

YOU ARE MEANT FOR HIM 28

YOU ARE SECURE 30

YOU ARE SET APART 32

YOU ARE SHELTERED 34

YOU ARE COMPLETE 36

YOU ARE ENOUGH 38

YOU ARE REDEEMED 40

YOU ARE PROMISED 42

YOU ARE GIVEN TIME 44

YOU ARE SOUGHT AFTER 46

YOU ARE RIGHT WHERE YOU NEED TO BE 48

YOU ARE ACCOMPANIED 50

YOU ARE BLESSED 52

YOU ARE GIVEN HIS SPIRIT 54

YOU ARE PROTECTED 56

YOU ARE SPOKEN TO	58
YOU ARE LIFTED	60
YOU ARE STRONG	62
YOU ARE HELD	64
YOU ARE SEEN	66
YOU ARE COURAGEOUS	68
YOU ARE HUMAN	70
YOU ARE AN OVERCOMER	72
YOU ARE LIGHT	74
YOU ARE COVERED	76
YOU ARE KNOWN	78
YOU ARE IMPERFECTLY PERFECT	80
YOU ARE WORTHY	82
YOU ARE SETTLED	84
YOU ARE DESIRED	86
YOU ARE STILL	88
YOU ARE RELIEVED	90
YOU ARE MADE FOR GRATITUDE	92
YOU ARE GIVEN GRACE	94
YOU ARE MADE WITH HIM IN MIND	96
YOU ARE SWEET	98
YOU ARE NOT FORGOTTEN	100
YOU ARE HIS	102
YOU ARE UNDERSTOOD	104
YOU ARE CHOSEN	106
YOU ARE DIFFERENT	108
YOU ARE CHANGED	110

Adi Welp

You Are Made New

2 Corinthians 5:17 – This means that anyone who belongs to Christ has become a new person. The old life is gone; a new life has begun.

You are made new, My child. The old has gone. The new has come – with Me. I am the source of your newness. I allow you to live again. With each breath, I fill your lungs with life. With each step, I fill your body with strength. With each beat, I fill your heart with joy. Your life in Me is rich. I set the refresh button on your life daily. Don't we all need a refresh? A refreshed mind free from earthly worries. A refreshed heart set on fire for a Savior. A refreshed being that is ready to serve. I will make you new each and every day for as long as you come to Me. Will you step into My presence today and accept the new you? Will you answer the knock on your heart? I am waiting for you. I am waiting to make you new.

Lord Jesus, thank You for a refresh. Lord knows I need to be made new daily. I am exhausted from the world and earthly things. I thank You, that in You, I am not who the world says I am. I am thankful that I am not called to do the things the world says to do. I am thankful that being made new means being the creation that You have called me to be. I am thankful that You give me new beginnings to do so. Help me to walk into this day knowing tomorrow is behind me and right now is in front of me. You are the Lord of the present. And in this present moment, Jesus, I am loved, strengthened, and worthy of this life. Lord Jesus, help my new creation to pour over into the hearts that You have chosen to be in my presence.

Notes

Adi Welp

You Are Rescued

Isaiah 46:4 – I will be your God throughout your lifetime – until your hair is white with age. I made you, and I will care for you. I will carry you along and save you.

Raise your head and hands up, My child. Like a child being scooped up in his father's big arms, you are My child, and I rescue you. Be comforted in My arms as I show you My rescue. You may think you can't be rescued. You're too far gone and that your rescue looks different from the girl next door. Ultimately, My rescue is the same for every believer. You all need to be rescued from worldly things, and you need it daily. Good thing I am a rescuer that brings you out of this world and into My light. See My face. And My arms around you. They are full of comfort, love, and peace. You are significant and worthy to Me. You always have been and always will be. As your feet hit the floor every morning, let Me sweep them up, My child. Let Me sweep you off your feet and rescue you. Rescue work is My favorite kind.

Lord Jesus, thank You for seeing me. You have not forgotten me. You hear every repeated cry from my heart even when I don't have the words. And most importantly, You don't just see and hear me, You rescue me. You rescue me. What beautiful words I can sing today. My rescuer is the God of the universe. All powerful. All knowing. And He holds me in His arms. Today, I am weightless in His arms. I am free from what was holding me down, and I go forth, rescued. I imagine You holding me in the palm of Your hand and carrying me through every situation I face. Your hand is strong and firm, yet gentle and leading. I know in Your hand, I am safe. Lord Jesus, help me to accept the gift of this rescue and rescuer each and every day.

Notes

You Are Made In The Image Of God

Ephesians 2:10 For we are God's masterpiece. He has created us anew in Christ Jesus, so we can do the good things he planned for us long ago.

My beautiful child. Oh, how I see such beauty in you. Outward beauty, yes, but you are so much more than that. You are My creation. My creation. My very breath was used to form you. Your heart beats in rhythm with Mine. Your lungs inhale My spirit. You were created with a purpose in mind. Your purpose comes alive when you remain close to Me, your creator. A painter does not leave his canvas before his best work is done. Just so, I will not leave you as you grow into who I created you to be. I am marvelous, bright, unimaginable, and you are made exceptional in Me. The world is not exceptional, My child. But you are. Just like a mirror, My image reflects onto you. The beauty I reflect in you is untouchable by the world's standards. Your beauty is untouchable, My child. Live in that truth.

Lord Jesus, thank You for making me beautiful. Thank You for making my heart and inner self beautiful. Because You are beautiful, I can see myself as beautiful in Your image. My beauty cannot be tamed. My beauty is a light to this world. In joy, in suffering, in loss, in peace, in chaos, and in calm, the light of my inner self does not dim. I will not let it dim, Lord. I will look into the mirror and see You shining through me, counting on me to be the very creation that this world needs. In You, I am created to do unimaginable and unfathomable things. You imprinted this promise on me the day I was conceived. As a tiny cell in my mother's womb, You painted my picture. Today, I hold the brush with You and make strokes towards finishing what You've started in me.

You Are: A Journal of His Voice

Notes

Adi Welp

You Are Fought For

Exodus 14:14 – The Lord himself will fight for you. Just stay calm.

My child, your battle is difficult. I know. I've been there. I've experienced loneliness, exclusion, abuse, loss, despair… a desperation so big that I've been left on My knees begging My Father to stop the battle. But, I have overcome. I am the overcomer. And when the overcomer stands with you, you will not fall. You must be still. You must let the overcomer hold you. You must let the overcomer fight. When you surrender the fight to the One who does the fighting, the battle is won. The battle is no longer yours. It's Mine. I will fight tooth and nail for you to give Me this battle you are facing. I will not give up on you because My Father did not give up on Me. Be still, My child, and let Me fight for you.

Lord Jesus, thank You for fighting for me. Wow. Those words… I am fought for. I would never have dreamed that my life is worth fighting for, yet here You stand. Lord, behind me, before me, surrounding me with Your angel armies. Help me to lay down my pride that keeps me holding onto this fight. Help me to lay down my fear that wonders what will happen if I let go. You know what will happen when I let go of the fight. Freedom. Freedom to watch the overcomer fight a battle I cannot win. I will never win. Only in You will I win this fight. Only in You will I overcome. Shhhhh. I am quiet, Lord. I am waiting. I am watching. Take this from my cup, Jesus.

Notes

Adi Welp

You Are Cared For

Exodus 16:4 – Then the Lord said to Moses, "Look, I'm going to rain down food from heaven for you. Each day the people can go out and pick up as much food as they need for that day..."

My child, the days seem long. At times, you feel like you can't catch your breath. Look up. Call on the One that provides your every need. You are not forgotten. In fact, you are thought about every second of every day. I delight in caring for you. I delight in giving you the very things you need for each day. An unexpected break, a hot coffee, a place to sleep, a friend, a note, a whisper telling you to lay down child and accept My care. Lean in and listen for My voice. I know what you need, and I give it to you. What you think you need may be different from what your inner self needs. I provide the stuff your soul needs. You cannot touch that. But don't worry, child. You will not go hungry. You will not go thirsty… in Me. You are cared for, My child. I care, and you are Mine.

Lord Jesus, thank You for meeting my every need. Thank You for providing me with daily bread. Your bread does not cause hunger or neglect but fullness and life. The things I use to take care of my needs only sustain me temporarily. But, You. You, Jesus, provide care that sustains me permanently. In Your word, in Your whispers throughout the day, I am full. Only You can sustain me when I can't breathe. Only You can fill me when I'm on empty. Only You can give me rest when the race feels impossible. Only You can speak life over me when I feel forgotten. I am not forgotten. I am loved and cared for by my creator. I am given a choice to take Your daily bread and let it nourish and change me. Today, I choose You to fulfill my every need.

Notes

Adi Welp

You Are Not Alone

Exodus 17:12 – Moses's arms soon became so tired he could no longer hold them up. So Aaron and Hur found a stone for him to sit on. Then they stood on each side of Moses, holding up his hands. So his hands held steady until sunset.

You are supported, My child. I am your rock. The rock you rest on when you are weary. The rock that does not weather, does not move, does not leave you in your struggle. I see your exhaustion. I meet you there, child. I pull up a seat and never leave your side. I not only stay, I send. I send others to be with you. To sit with you. To lift your tired spirit. To meet you in your mess. Be watchful and listen to the ones I send. Do not hang with your head so low that you miss them or dismiss their invitation to endure. Endure with them. Look to your left, look to your right, and smile. See how they hold you. How I hold you. You are not alone, and you will endure, My child. You are one of Mine… and you are in great company.

Lord Jesus, thank You for sitting with me. Thank You for calling me friend, calling me Yours, calling me worthy. When I call out to my God, You do not reign from afar but meet me in my mess. You sit. You listen. You send. You send me people. People that are like me – messy. But, also people that share qualities of You. People that don't leave when I break down. People that listen through my cries. People that are supportive enough to not leave me how they found me. I am never alone. Help me to hear the voice of You in my heart and in the voices of people that approach me today. And if I feel alone, one word is all it takes. I will repeat Jesus, Jesus, Jesus – my lifeline and my rock.

Notes

Adi Welp

You Are In His Vision

Habakkuk 2:3 – This vision is for a future time. It describes the end, and it will be fulfilled. If it seems slow in coming, wait patiently, for it will surely take place. It will not be delayed.

You play an important role in My story, child. I envisioned what you would do for Me since the moment I made you. I envisioned you to be a most precious part of this world. Keep sight of the vision, My child. Keep your eyes up and ahead on who holds your vision. What you see today is not a reflection of what tomorrow will be. What you fear today is not a guarantee of your future. Your vision is in My hands. And let Me tell you child, it is perfect. I am perfect, and what I have envisioned for you is perfect. You've been waiting for Me to reveal it to you. I see you struggling in the waiting. I see you wrestling with Me. Wrestle away, My child. I can handle your wrestling because I am here to tell you, your wrestling is worth it. What I have prepared for you will be fulfilled. It will come to fruition. Write down your vision and believe it. Believe that I hold it and am waiting to bless you with it in My perfect timing.

Lord Jesus, thank You for the vision You have perfected for my life. Thank You that I am not in charge of it, but You are. For You know me better than I know myself. Reveal my deepest desires in Your timing. Make them known to me when the timing aligns with Your story. Your story. This isn't about me. Help me to remember, it's about You. My timing is irrelevant. Your timing is everything. Your timing blesses Your story, Your people, Your purpose – help me to remember that when the timing is right, more people will be blessed. Help me to keep showing up in the waiting. In the waiting, help me to keep coming back, keep wrestling You, and keep strengthening my belief. Your best work is done in the waiting.

Notes

Adi Welp

You Are Heard

1 John 5:15 – And since we know he hears us when we make our requests, we also know that he will give us what we ask for.

I hear you, My child. I hear you. You are tired. You are desperate. You are out of breath. Out of breath from running a race you cannot win – alone. Cry out to Me. Make your requests known. Sing them from the rooftops. Scream them from the valleys. No request is too big or too small. When you don't have the words, say My name – Jesus. Jesus. Jesus. Over and over. I long to hear you say My name. I fill in the blanks. Jesus. Jesus. Jesus. "Yes, child?" Jesus. Jesus. Jesus. "I am here, child." Jesus. Jesus. Jesus. "You are safe, child." Jesus. Jesus. Jesus. "You are so loved, child." Jesus. Jesus. Jesus. "I will never leave you, child." Jesus. Jesus. Jesus. My name has meaning. I know what you need. You don't have to say another word. My name alone is power. A cry that I will never get tired of hearing. A cry that has more impact than you can ever imagine. I hear you. And I meet you where you are.

Lord Jesus, thank You for hearing me. Thank You for listening to understand and not to respond. Thank You for Your affirmations. Thank You for Your assurance. My cries aren't perfect. More often than not, I don't have the words. I find myself stumbling, repeating, and losing my train of thought as I speak to You. Between tears. Between a mental load that seems unbearable. Between anxiousness about the future. Between exhaustion from the day. There's so much that impacts my ability to focus on You in prayer, and for that, I'm sorry, Jesus. But You hear. You know what I'm trying to say before I say it. You hear the cry of my heart. A heart that wants You, needs You, and would do anything to have someone truly listen to her. My Father. My Friend. Jesus. Jesus. Jesus.

Notes

Adi Welp

You Are Cleansed

Lamentations 3:22-23 – The faithful love of the Lord never ends! His mercies never cease. Great is his faithfulness; his mercies begin afresh each morning.

Look up, My child. Feel the rain hit your cheek. Down it slides. Cool. Refreshing. Breathe in. Breathe out. Let My presence wash over you. You are cleansed each morning. My mercies are new. Feel Me still your soul and quiet your mind. You are ready to take a step forward into the day. Take a step under the umbrella, and let My grace cover you today. Until you need a rinse. There will always be opportunities to cleanse yourself. Whenever you ask, you will be cleansed. Washed from the sins of the day. From the chaos, fear, sadness, and whatever else keeps you from Me. After I cleanse you, find Me under the umbrella ready to give you life. I have forgotten about the dirt that was washed off. You are cleansed and ready to walk hand in hand with Me. Will you join Me, My child?

Lord Jesus, thank You for Your mercy and grace that wash over me. Just like soap and water, they cleanse me and make me shine like new. My soul is calmed and ready to walk with You. What a feeling. It's indescribable. I feel light. Weightless, in fact. The world does not seem so heavy as I am cleansed and covered by You. By Your umbrella that does not bend when the wind blows. You paid it all. I did nothing. I earned nothing. The only title I own that makes me worthy of Your cleansing is "child of God." You offer the rain. Again. And again. And again. And I'll keep coming back. I need the rain often. Cleanse me, Father.

You Are: A Journal of His Voice

Notes

Adi Welp

You Are Filled

John 4:14 – Jesus replied, "Anyone who drinks this water will soon become thirsty again. But those who drink the water I give will never be thirsty again. It becomes a fresh, bubbling spring within them, giving them eternal life."

Slow down, My child. You run here. You run there. Your mind races. How often do your thoughts land on Me? How often do they land on others? I am here to give you a hard truth, My child. You will never keep up with the pace of life. You will run yourself into the ground if you don't come back to the very well that gives you living water every single day. You need Me to settle your mind. Your heart. Your soul. I fill you and give you something you long for… grace. Grace for not finishing the to-do list. Grace for not staying late at work so you can have supper with your family instead. Grace for saving those dishes or laundry for another day. Life is busy, but you don't have to be, child. Feel My grace wash over you. When you feel that you didn't do enough in a day, know that you did more than enough, My child. You did. You did when you met Me at the well.

Lord Jesus, thank You for filling my cup every day. I run and run and run. My mind goes and goes and goes. Both are races. Life feels like one big race. But it doesn't have to. Not with You leading the pack. You fill me with living water. Water that does not run dry. Water that quenches my every thirst. You fill in my gaps. I have gaps, Lord – oh, do I have gaps. You don't question them. You just fill them. You fill them as long as I ask. As long as I keep coming to Your well, You will fill my gaps and prepare me with the exact amount of water I need for the next day. No more, no less. I will choose to use my water to pour into others. As You pour into me, I will pour into others. The more I pour out of my cup, the more that is in my cup. It doesn't make sense, yet it makes all the sense in the world. Meet me at the well, my Jesus.

You Are: A Journal of His Voice

Notes

Adi Welp

You Are Meant For Him

Luke 5:16 – But Jesus often withdrew to the wilderness for prayer.

When I say you are meant for Me, My child, I mean it. You are meant to sit alone with Me. In the quiet. In solitude. And frequently. The world will pull you. But you aren't meant for it. You aren't meant to spend every hour of the day on a hamster wheel while I patiently wait for you to sit at My table. I'm here. I'm available. I long for you to join Me. "I'm too busy." "I don't have time." "I can't sit down." I've heard them all. But listen here, child. When you are busy, you need Me even more. You need Me the most when your life is out of control. The only way you will combat the lies of the world is by slipping away with Me. 5 minutes, 10 minutes, an hour. Give Me what you can. I will give you what you can't gain with any other "thing" you try to feed your soul – meaning in your moments, joy in your trials, and peace in your being.

Lord Jesus, thank You for waiting for me in the silence. My heart cries when I think of You, my best friend, sitting at a table alone, waiting for me to join. I am guilty of excuses, and I need mental toughness, Lord Jesus. Help me to resist my human nature of excuses daily and sit where I am meant to be – with You. Help me to walk like Jesus walked, slipping away to a secluded place to pray even when the world was constantly knocking on His door. He knew the only way to gain strength, purpose, meaning, joy, peace, and love was to sit with His Father. He knew the only way to have more time was to give it up. He knew that the only way to an abundant life was a surrendered and still soul. Help me to surrender my time. For the sake of my soul, I will sit with You, Jesus. Right where I'm meant to be.

Notes

You Are Secure

Job 11:18 – Having hope will give you courage. You will be protected and will rest in safety.

My child, I've got you. Melt into My arms for a little while. Then, stand tall. Courageous. Confident. Look around you and feel My security overcome you. I hold you up. Take steps forward. One. Two. Three. Feel My arms underneath yours? Feel your steps lighten as you walk with Me? No longer heavy but free. There is hope in this kind of walk we take together. Hope for lighter days. Brighter days. I am the God that tells the sun when to rise and the stars when to shine. Shine now, My child. When you are secure in Me, you shine the brightest. Your light cannot be dimmed. Your spirit cannot be contained. You are hope for the insecure. Because you were once there. You were once one of them. Not anymore, My child. You are secure. You have a place at My table. You have a spot at My side as we walk. You are safe and secure from all the days behind you and all the days ahead.

Lord Jesus, thank You for securing my place next to You. Thank You for lifting me out of my insecurity, my anxiousness, my fear and calling me chosen. Secure. Yours. In all honesty, my heart gets heavy some days. I feel the weight on my shoulders increase. One thought of You – my safe place, my security, the person I trust more than anyone – and my soul dances. I feel light, free, and safe no matter what is happening around me. You help me walk in confidence. You help me be bold. You help me walk with light steps knowing who walks beside me. The walk is hard. There's no way around it. But knowing who walks with me makes all the difference. I will look to my side and smile today as I walk in bold confidence.

Notes

Adi Welp

You Are Set Apart

Leviticus 20:26 – You must be holy because I, the Lord, am holy. I have set you apart from all other people to be my very own.

Dear child, I hope you know when I created you, I had a distinct purpose in mind. You were created like no one else. You were formed in My image, with My breath, with Me in your heart. I love everything about you. When I saw you for the first time. When I heard your heart beat strongly. When you took your first breath. When you opened your eyes to the world. When your unique voice screamed a mighty cry like a lion. I looked down and smiled. I was so proud. I was so in love. You were fearless, strong, and beautiful. But, you needed something. You needed to be held in comforting arms. Your earthly parents took on that role at first, but as you continue through life, I take on that role. You need Me, My child. You need Me. Only I set you apart. Being set apart means experiencing fullness in your life with My peace, joy, and love. It means daring to live like no one around you. For you were not meant for this place. You never were. Your purpose is for something greater. For someone greater. Set yourself apart by meeting with Me, and I will show you all that you are meant for. My child, I can't begin to tell you how much I have waiting for you.

Lord Jesus, thank You for setting me apart. For calling me Yours. For calling me to greatness. Your greatness looks different than what the world defines as "greatness." But Lord, I am not worried about the world. I know You have immeasurable blessings waiting for me as I set myself apart with You and the way You have called me to go. Thank You for creating me so detailed, so intentionally, so loved. When the children You have so carefully crafted come to You, I cannot imagine the joy You feel inside. Like a child coming home to his empty nest parents. Lead my heart and mind to come to You daily. On days when I am stubborn and think I've got it on my own, remind me that I don't. I never will. Remind me that coming together with You will in turn set me apart from this world. Not as I will but as You will.

Notes

You Are Sheltered

Matthew 7:25 – Though the rain comes in torrents and the floodwaters rise and the winds beat against that house, it won't collapse because it is built on bedrock.

My child, come back to your sheltering place. You get busy. You waste time worrying. You drown yourself in productivity. The storm still rages amidst your ever busy body trying to make your storm stop or even just calm down a little. My presence is a safe place. I cover you from the drops. I shield you from the wind. I comfort you from the cold. I drown out the loud cracking of the thunder. When you meet with Me, you hear a still, small voice. Like a bird chirping at the end of a rain. You feel peace. Like cuddling up on the couch with a cozy blanket to view the storm from the inside. You see, My child, storms come in all sizes. A never ceasing misty rain on a windy spring day. A 6 minute downpour in the heat of summer. A tumultuous thunder and lightning war in the night sky. They don't discriminate, and there's no telling when you'll come in contact with one. But when you do, know who shelters you. Know who keeps you standing tall. Know whose hand you hold. If you know who, you know your storm has met its match.

Lord Jesus, thank You for the shelter You provide in my storms. Lord, my storms vary. Sometimes by the day. I get moody – mad, sad, exhausted, confused, happy. Yet, sometimes, the storms are real heartaches, hardships, things I wish I didn't have to go through. You meet me in every one. From my minor storms, to my major storms, You never leave me. No matter how miniscule my mishaps may seem. Because if it's important to me, it's important to You. But Lord, I also am learning that the more I come to meet with You, the less scary my storms seem. I am able to stand tall. I am able to withstand the winds. I am able to feel peace at each new crack of thunder. My house is built on rock. My house stands strong. My house knows who built it. As for me and my house, we will cling to You.

Notes

Adi Welp

You Are Complete

John 15:11 – I have told you these things so that you will be filled with my joy. Yes, your joy will overflow!

Come away with Me, My child. Practice resting with Me. I want to whisper songs of joy in your heart. I want to breathe completeness in your soul. What if there was no life-giving escape to the daily grind? Day after day you worked, you exerted energy, you depleted your thoughts. Then, you went to the next day to do it all over again. And the next day. And the next day. You jumped on social media for a quick fix, but you found yourself in the same position the very next day. It does not have to be like this. But sadly, it often is. My child, I am life. I am whole. I am complete. Everything in your soul is made complete through Me. Your joy is complete. You can look at any situation with positivity. Your peace is complete. You can face any battle with comfort. Your love is complete. You can be completely yourself in front of Me and that is when My love pours out of you best. Please come to Me. Weekly, daily, hourly, every minute. Think of how complete your life would be if My presence filled every minute as you completed each day.

Lord Jesus, thank You for the gift of wholeness in You. Nothing missing. Nothing lacking. Just completeness in You. Best gift ever. And it's free, Lord Jesus – thank You that it is free. Help me to be reminded of that completeness often by guiding my thoughts to You and Your word. When I am feeling worthless, I run to You. When I am feeling like I don't measure up, I run to You. When I am feeling incomplete, I run to You. That is the answer for everything missing in my life. Running to You. Your arms are outstretched. I can see it, Lord. I am running into Your open arms. That hug. Oh, that hug wraps me in complete joy, peace, and love. I do not need anything more. I do not seek anything more. I do not want anything more than completeness in You, Jesus.

You Are: A Journal of His Voice

Notes

Adi Welp

You Are Enough

1 Kings 17:12 – But she said, "I swear by the Lord your God that I don't have a single piece of bread in the house. And I have only a handful of flour left in the jar and a little cooking oil in the bottom of the jug…"

My child, I don't use you when you are already complete. When you've got it all figured out. That doesn't even make sense, child. Why would you need Me when you have it all together? I use you when you are broken. Confused. Defeated. When you come to Me with all you have even though it doesn't feel like much. A little here and a little there. Don't you know that I will take your "littles" and make them into a masterpiece. Your "littles" are enough. Give Me your handful of flour. Give Me your olive oil. And watch Me work. Watch Me change, "I'm not good at that", "I'm too this, I'm too that", "I'm not her" into "I am enough." As you are, you are enough. Enough to do this job. Enough to take this risk. Enough to form that relationship. Enough to dwell in the presence of God, unashamed. My child, you are enough because I am everything.

Lord Jesus, thank You for calling me enough. Thank You for anointing me with gifts that are enough for You and Your heaven. I may not ever live up to the standards of the world, but Lord Jesus, Your standards are even higher, and You say I've met them. You say I measure up. You say I have everything I need. You say I am worthy. Lord, those truths set me free and call me higher. If I am enough for the King of Kings, I will stand tall in my daily routines to meet You with all that I have. I will bring my flour. I will bring my olive oil. I'm not a finished product, but I am here. I am waiting for You to take what I have and be enough in me.

Notes

Adi Welp

You Are Redeemed

Matthew 28:6 – He isn't here! He is risen from the dead, just as he said would happen. Come, see where his body was lying.

Look up to the heavens, My child. You will find Me. I came down to this broken world. I gave you ways in which to live. I ascended back to My true home. A home that is yours too if you choose to live and follow Me. I am not here physically, but I am still with you. I come down to meet you as often as you need. I will keep humbling Myself to help you. To teach you. To love you. That's the love of Me and My Father. It knows no end. I will keep coming back for you. I have defeated the darkness, just as I said. Believe Me now when I speak truth to you. That you are chosen, just as I said. That you are forgiven, just as I said. That you are loved, just as I said. That you are a precious child of the King, just as I said. That you are redeemed, just as I said. I did the impossible so life with you could be possible, My child.

Lord Jesus, thank You for calling me redeemed. Thank You for enduring an unimaginable death all while thinking of me on that cross – "You, (name), are one of Mine. This is for you." I am humbled, awestruck, and have a limited capacity to wrap my mind around the magnitude of that moment, Lord Jesus, but thank You that You remind me of all the truths that came from that moment daily. The truths that I can sing to myself and future generations that I am chosen, forgiven, loved, and redeemed. These truths are right in front of me in the Bible. Every day I can choose to gain insight on what that moment in history truly meant for me. I am no longer a slave to the darkness because my Jesus beats it every time. Not just some, but every time, for as long as I ask Him to. Thank you for redeeming every moment of my life and bringing light to every moment from here on.

You Are: A Journal of His Voice

Notes

Adi Welp

You Are Promised

Numbers 23:19 – ...Has he ever spoken and failed to act? Has he ever promised and not carried it through?

In My house, you are promised life, My child. A life that is full, beautiful, and rich in joy. You are promised the desires of your heart. As long as they come from Me and do not have separate motives, you are promised these desires, My child. You are promised eternity. A place of rest, abundance, peace, and everlasting love, My child. A place that seems unfathomable in today's world. Since you were knit together in your mother's womb, I had great promises for you. They are waiting to be uncovered and longing to be found by you. Find Me first. Uncover My face. And My voice. There you will find your ultimate longings and promises that are beyond what you can imagine. There is not a word I speak that will be dismissed. There is not a promise I will not fulfill when you find Me. My promise is sacred, and it is for your taking, My child.

Lord Jesus, thank You for Your never-ending promises. Not a promise of Yours to me goes unfulfilled. Not a word spoken to me is hollow. Your words are true. They hold value. Your promises for me are good. They give me peace. They give me hope. They give me joy. I am excited to uncover Your promises. Seek me and find me, Lord Jesus. Discipline me so that I would seek and find You. That Your face would be all I see so that I can follow You. When I lay down my life to follow You, I see Your promises revealed and Your plan for my life unraveled. Your promises are woven together beautifully to create my story, and my Jesus, You do not miss a detail. Let me in on Your promises for me.

Notes

Adi Welp

You Are Given Time

Ecclesiastes 3:1 – For everything there is a season, a time for every activity under heaven.

Stop looking at the clock, My child. "If I could get this done in that hour and that done in that hour, then I would be happy. Then I would feel productive. Then I would be done with my to-do list." Lie, lie, lie. Stop worrying about your agenda, and focus on Mine, My child. I have placed people for you to love in your day, every day. They are in need of the gifts you have to give. If you are thinking about your to-do list and time, you will miss them. They will pass you by. And passing them by one day leads to a week. And a week turns into months. And months turn into years. Before you know it, My child, you are at the end of your life, wondering what your purpose is. Your purpose is to look in anticipation for the people you can love today. Love them fully. Love them kindly. And love them well. Then you will look back and wonder, "What more can I do with all my time?" – rather than, "I don't have enough time." You will always be given enough time to complete your mission for Me. My time is sufficient for you. Come to Me, and you will find more time than you could ever spend, My child.

Lord Jesus, thank You for this truth that You are the giver of my time. I look at a day – 24 hours – and think, that's not enough. It may not be enough for my agenda, but when will it ever? It's not about me. If I constantly think that You give me 24 hours to do what I want, I will consistently be disappointed. However, it will be enough for Your agenda. Help me to put aside my wants and desires for my day and instead focus on the ones that align with Your will. First and foremost, spending time quietly with You. It is Your daily will for me to sit in Your presence, and through it, I will find the answer to what to do with the time You have given me for that day. Even if it's to rest. Even if it's to play on the floor with my baby. Even if it's to clean the bed sheets. Even if it's to visit that family member I have been too "busy" for. Even if it's to work… none of it is too minor or too major for You. You will show up. And You will provide enough time for the things that align with Your agenda.

You Are: A Journal of His Voice

Notes

Adi Welp

You Are Sought After

Deuteronomy 7:7-8 – The Lord did not set his heart on you and choose you because you were more numerous than other nations, for you were the smallest of all nations! Rather, it was simply that the Lord loves you...

I chose your heartbeat, My child. The color of your eyes. The joy in your smile. I chose how tall you would be. How strong you would be. How I would look at you in awe, wondering how I could have ever made such a perfect being. And I would choose you all over again. My heart is set on you. You were made for needing My heartbeat. Needing My breath in your lungs. Needing My spirit in your days. My child, don't go at it alone. You can't, and you were never meant to. It is difficult to comprehend, child, but I will never stop seeking you. When you are at the highest of highs or lowest of lows, I seek you. I want you to know My voice like you know your baby's cry. When you hear it, you rush urgently to meet your child. I will keep seeking you until you have that same sense of urgency when you hear My voice. Let's choose each other to walk through life with.

Lord Jesus, thank You for continuously seeking me when I don't get it right. When I open social media before I open my bible. When I call my mom before I call out to You. When You aren't the first person my mind goes to when I'm on a mountain or in a valley. Thank You, Jesus, for Your grace, but I also ask that You would transform my mind so that I seek You in those moments. As much as You seek me, I want to seek You. I want to know Your voice like my baby's cry. I want to be quick to hear what You have to say instead of what the world has to say. I want my heart to be set on You just like You set Your heartbeat in me. I am nothing special without You, but with You, I am everything this world needs.

Notes

You Are Right Where You Need To Be

James 3:17 – But the wisdom from above is first of all pure. It is also peace loving, gentle at all times, and willing to yield to others. It is full of mercy and the fruit of good deeds. It shows no favoritism and is always sincere.

Breathe in and out. In this space, with Me, is where you need to be. You look to the future, My child. You wonder what is next. Your mind gets wrapped up in the anxiety of the unknown, yet it hopes for better days to come. But, My child, the grass is not greener. It does not grow taller over there. You sitting with Me, yes, that is when you grow. Your joy does not come from your circumstance changing but instead from you changing. So don't pursue situational changes. Pursue heart changes. Mind changes. Soul changes. Changes that overtake you in the best way possible and that only come from gaining wisdom. Seek the purest form of wisdom, heavenly wisdom. For the wisdom I whisper onto those who wish for it is truth. It leads you to right where you need to be.

Lord Jesus, thank You for reminding me to receive Your wisdom today. I pray this wisdom is gentle enough to give me grace yet strong enough to nudge me onto the path that could only be created by You. Lord, when I am unsure, when I feel the outside world rushing around me, help me to rest in You – right where I need to be. I am a human being, not a human doing. I was made to be with You. By being with You, I gain wisdom that surpasses my age. I gain a calling that is unfathomable to me right now. I gain a peace that is unmoved. Help this wisdom that You instill in me, be in Your absolute purest form so that everything I do is done in Your name. Your name. Your precious, holy name. You and I together. It's the best place to be.

Notes

Adi Welp

You Are Accompanied

Deuteronomy 19:8-9 – And if the Lord your God enlarges your territory, as he swore to your ancestors, and gives you all the land he promised them, you must designate three additional cities of refuge. (He will give you this land if you are careful to obey all the commands I have given you – if you always love the Lord your God and walk in his ways.)

My child, lean in. I am working to give you My promises. My promises may not be what you have asked for, but they are what you need. Let's walk together. Hand in hand. Is your soul immediately comforted? Mine is. Like a baby laid on the chest of his mama. All is right in the world. There is no doubt, fear, confusion, or loneliness. A baby knows, this is the one. She is mine. Just like I want you to know, this is my Father. He is mine. Let Me tell you My child, walking on your own will lead to doubt, fear, confusion, and loneliness. Those have no place on My path. My path is a walk of assurance, friendship, love, and grace. I will do everything I can to meet you on your path and steer you toward Mine. You may think your path is too messy for Me, but child, do you not know that I live in the mess? It is in the mess where desperation causes total surrender to letting Me in. Let Me accompany you in your mess, My child.

Lord Jesus, thank You for going before me, behind me, beside me, and all around me. You give me a simple command – walk in My ways. Walk with Me. Yet, I complicate it. I think I can do it on my own. I think my strength, grace, and power are sufficient… when in truth, for my whole life, the only way I am where I am today is because of You. Because of Your love for me at the cross, I am saved. Because of Your grace, I am washed clean each day and told not to look back at my sins. Because of Your strength in me, I get the privilege to raise a child in this broken world. Because of Your boldness in me, I am able to take leaps I never thought I could. And because of Your faithfulness to me, I am guided through unknown waters. Lord Jesus, I am so blessed. Not necessarily because of my life circumstances but because of who lives in me and whose ways I choose to walk in. I will let You accompany me in my mess.

Notes

Adi Welp

You Are Blessed

Deuteronomy 28:2-6 – You will experience all these blessings if you obey the Lord your God: ...Wherever you go and whatever you do, you will be blessed.

I am the giver of all blessings. I patiently wait to hand them out to you and watch you take delight in them, My child. Blessing you comes naturally. Effortlessly. It brings Me the greatest joy. I just ask, child, that you follow Me. Know My word like the back of your hand. Be so in tune with My voice that it is the only whisper you hear. Once you surrender, obey, follow – watch how your life changes. Move but only your faith muscle to receive the blessings I have waiting. Stop striving. Stop thinking you are earning them. It is not about you. It is about obeying every whisper I put on your heart and then watching as I go to work. Watch as I orchestrate the details of your life far better than you could imagine. Watch as I bless you with everything I have. Come into My presence, so you can go out with My blessings.

Lord Jesus, thank You for the blessings You have given me, are giving me, and have yet to give me. I think I know the blessings my family needs, but I don't. All the blessings I have in my mind are self-seeking. They don't bring You into the equation. They are misleading and not blessings at all if they do not involve You. Help me to shift my mind towards sitting instead of striving. Obeying instead of accomplishing. Surrendering instead of laboring. When I sit, obey, and surrender, now that's when I am blessed. Sitting with God? Obeying His word? Surrendering control? Some of those seem simple, but they are the most difficult actions in a self-centered and self-seeking world. Help me to be different. Breathe into me, my God. I want to be different and blessed.

Notes

Adi Welp

You Are Given His Spirit

2 Timothy 1:7 – For God has not given us a spirit of fear and timidity, but of power, love, and self-discipline.

My child, I breathe My spirit into open hearts. Hearts that are eager and hungry for growth. You see, when My spirit is within you, change happens. Walls are down. Eyes are opened. Ears are understanding. Hearts are softened. You need to be all in, My child. All too often, I see My children want My spirit. They yearn for a different way. They don't want to keep spinning their wheels. They are seeking a lighter burden… but, they are holding onto parts of them and parts of their dreams that I so desperately want to overtake. My child, I want all of your dreams to come true too, but if you would give Me all of you, I could show you that the dreams and things ahead of you are beautiful, unthinkable, and remarkable. They are blessings only received when you let Me embrace you fully with My spirit. My spirit is power against your enemies. My spirit is love without condemnation. My spirit is sound judgment for all your questions and decisions. My spirit is a gift. Let It come alive in you.

Lord Jesus, thank You for offering me the gift of Your spirit. When I sit down to reflect on what that truly means – to have the spirit of God breathed onto me, it is difficult to comprehend. God can give 'little me" the gifts to view the world like He does, love like He loves, act like He acts, and speak life like He speaks? If that is true, Lord, I am eager and hungry for it. And You of all people know I need it. A difficult day overtook me this week. I was anxious, fearful, sad, and felt so much guilt. It was a moment of feeling completely lost. A breakdown. Like a baby without his mother. Repeating this verse as I laid in my bed settled my heart. Peace flowed into the room. My Father was with me. I can imagine You holding me tight, wiping my tears, and pulling my hair back to see my face. Lord, that image occurs often. So many of Your children, including me, need Your spirit to overcome those days. To reshape our thinking. And soften our hearts to Your whispers. "I love you, My child. You are Mine. My spirit goes with you."

Notes

Adi Welp

You Are Protected

Joshua 10:8 – "Do not be afraid of them," the Lord said to Joshua, "for I have given you victory over them. Not a single one of them will be able to stand up to you."

I wrap My strong arms around you in protection, My child. Not just to keep your physical body safe but to keep your heart and mind safe – from the enemy, from lies, from pain, from fear, and from the world. No, this does not mean you won't have heartache, but listen to My words, My child. Listen when I say, "Not one of them will be able to stand against you." Not one. That means zero. Zilch. Nada. Not one lie, fear, or thing of this world will be able to stand against you. Joshua eagerly and bravely fought battles he shouldn't have faced. He wasn't equipped. He wasn't prepared. He wasn't great. Alone. That's the key word. Alone – alone, he gets beat every time. But, My child, when his heart was on Me. When he came to Me for his decisions. When he looked to Me for every move. When he asked Me boldly in faith for radical things like the sun to stand still, game over. The story was changed. He was equipped. He was prepared. He was great. I tell you repeatedly, and I won't stop telling you, My child. Do not be afraid. I've got this.

Lord Jesus, thank You for Your mighty protection. Your strong arms and Your gentle heart protect me both physically and mentally. Thank You for helping me to face the unknown boldly with courage and faith. Reading this truth makes me wonder why I ever question You. My guards fall. My fear fades. My heart is opened to receive Your endless protection over my life. "Do not be afraid," You say. I won't. I can't. I don't have time for that because You're calling me into something greater. Something I may not know now but someday will. Something I may miss if I focus on the fear. Lord, You've got me. Lord, You've equipped me. Lord, You've prepared me for this exact moment in time. I won't stop finding You in my every day because, as You said, with You, game over.

Notes

Adi Welp

You Are Spoken To

Joshua 21:45 – Not a single one of all the good promises the Lord had given to the family of Israel was left unfulfilled; everything he had spoken came true.

I have big promises for you, My child. Promises that I cannot wait to reveal to you. Keep walking in step with Me. That is how you unlock them. Lean when I lean. Move forward when I move forward. Pause when I pause. You're doing it, child. You're living in My rhythms. And on My time. My promises are beautiful and true. I hand them out as you faithfully obey. Isn't it a one-of-a-kind dance you and I shuffle to? Today, sit in My unconditional promises. The promises I offer to you daily. I promise you peace. A peace that stills your soul. Serenity. Sweet serenity. I promise you joy. A joy that warms your heart with an overflow of abundance and gratitude. Your cup is full. I promise you love. A love that is vast and sincere. Feel My arms around you. The same arms that made the ocean wide. You are My gift. You are My treasure. You are promised all that I am when you give Me all that you are.

Lord Jesus, thank You for this gift of today. I am not promised each day, but Lord, I am promised You in each day that You choose to give me. The promise of You is peace, joy, and love. "Everything was fulfilled." Everything. That is a powerful statement. And, it gives me such hope. The world does the opposite for me, but You say everything is possible, and everything is fulfilled in You. When You formed me in my mother's womb, You said, "This one. I have big promises for this one." I get goosebumps thinking about it. I imagine You say that to all Your children. Sadly, all of Your children do not step into the rhythms of Your dance to unlock their promises. But this one, Lord. This one will follow. This one will dance. This one will shine. She is fulfilled. Because You fill her. You don't fail me. You fulfill me.

Notes

Adi Welp

You Are Lifted

Judges 6:15-16 – "But Lord," Gideon replied, "how can I rescue Israel? My clan is the weakest in the whole tribe of Manasseh, and I am the least in my entire family!" The Lord said to him, "I will be with you..."

"But I will be with you, My child." That new job you have. But, I will be with you. That exhaustion you feel after your baby cries out for the fifth time in one night. But, I will be with you. That big move you have to make for your family. But, I will be with you. That leap of faith. But, I will be with you. But, God. Yes, Me. I will sustain you. I will lift you to new heights. You will not be alone. You were made to stand on that rock, to move that mountain, to withstand that flood. You are lifted high, My child. No matter your status, your race, your age, your abilities. I am sending you. I am sending you to do the hard thing. To do the thing that has been nudging your heart for years. To do the thing that seems impossible, silly, and even crazy. But, God. Yes, Me. "But I will be with you." I lift you to places that only I can see. And what a beautiful view I see in you, My child.

Lord Jesus, thank You for Your constant reminder of how close You really are. Thank You that I am reminded that You take my insecurities, fears, and worries, just like Gideon's doubts, and say, "But God, My child. I am sending you." You didn't choose that more qualified or more put-together woman for "that thing" in my life. You said, "You, My child. You. You are the one to do it." And You did not only call me out, but You said, "But I will be with you." I will take a step onto Your feet, Jesus. As a father dances around the living room with his daughter. The daughter does not fear falling or failure. Her daddy holds her. She feels light as a feather, strong, and daring on her daddy's feet. Let's do "that thing" together. Please do all the heavy lifting.

You Are: A Journal of His Voice

Notes

Adi Welp

You Are Strong

1 Samuel 1:15 – "...But I am very discouraged, and I was pouring out my heart to the Lord..."

My child, My loved one. Your voice is one I love. I long to hear it. Pour it out. Pour out your fears. Your insecurities. Your failures. Your worries. You see, My child, pouring them out does not benefit Me. I already know what you fear and worry about. I already know. Pouring them out gives you a safe place to cry out to the only one who can do anything about your situation. I'm sorry, My child, but your spouse, your mom, your dad, your friends, your sister and brother do not have control over your situation. As much as you want them to. As much as you cry out to them to change your circumstance. Child, they do not have the power. You do not have the power. My child, cry out to Me. I have the power. I have the wisdom. I have the will to change. And, if I do not change your circumstance, I will change you. I will change your heart, your mind, your thoughts. Your mourning will turn into dancing. Your fear will turn into peace. And, your worry will turn into gratitude. My child, I have you covered. Pour out your heart to Me and see what I can do.

Lord Jesus, thank You for being a safe place to cry out. Thank You for being a gracious God that loves me despite my continuous worries and fears. You know the end story. Nothing surprises You. If I would just lay down my control. Lay down my fears. Lay down the pressure to have answers to everything. The thing holding me back from fullness and freedom in You is myself. I get in the way. I want to control, to fix, to respond. But Lord, You want me to pause. To surrender. To cry out. To watch and see what You do. Lord Jesus, help me to have a prayerful heart like Hannah. A heart that runs to You when disaster strikes. A heart that is pure, that is raw, that is open. Lord, hear my cries from a place of desperation. That is how my cries feel sometimes, Lord. Desperate. You welcome desperation. In my weakest, You are strongest. Woah. So I don't need to feel ashamed or out of control at my weakest. There is a God in me who is at His strongest. And Your strongest, Lord, is all I need. Help me to let that sink in today.

Notes

You Are Held

Colossians 1:17 – He existed before anything else, and he holds all creation together.

Let's embrace, My child. Let your guard down. Feel your body become limp in My arms. You are not too heavy for Me. You fit perfectly in My loving arms. But all of a sudden… there you go. You resist. A little here. A little there. The world calls, and you listen. You believe the lies. You sit with the fear. You accept the anxiety. I compete in this tug-of-war game for you. For you, My beloved child. I made you. I know you better than you know yourself. And I hold together the pieces of your life. The pieces that feel broken, afraid, exhausted, and chaotic. Your marriage. Your family dynamics. Your kids. Your fears, doubts, dreams, and goals. I hold them all together in this perfect story of you. I came first, and I thought there should be a you. Yes, you. So walk in that confidence. Hold on to Me tight. I will never lose the silly tug-of-war game when it comes to you.

Lord Jesus, thank You for holding the pieces of my life. They seem all over the place. One moment, I'm fine, and within hours, things may change. For the better – or for the worse. That's the reality of life. I don't get to choose what my day presents itself with. But I can choose to be held by the One who holds all things together. You turn the page with me on each day. You see what is ahead of me. You celebrate my victories. You share in my joy. You smile like the proud, proud Father that You are. But, You also see when the page ahead is rocky and rough. You know when I will need more of You. You see before I even know, and You deliver. More strength, more grace, more patience, more love. Whatever is sufficient for the moment, You hold, and You give. Lord, help me to lean into Your embrace in all situations. Your arms don't stop holding me, so Lord, may my arms hold You right back.

You Are: A Journal of His Voice

Notes

Adi Welp

You Are Seen

1 Samuel 16:7 – But the Lord said to Samuel, "Don't judge by his appearance or height, for I have rejected him. The Lord doesn't see things the way you see them. People judge by outward appearance, but the Lord looks at the heart."

My child, I look at you and see a masterpiece. A work that only My hands are capable of. I see your beautiful exterior, child, but to Me, your interior is far more precious. I see you for you. For your hopes, your fears, your dreams, your trials, and every tear. I see when your heart leaps for joy and when it rips with hurt. I see what you are after. What you love the most. What you seek the most. I see when it's Me. I see when it's not Me. You are good, My child. You were made from good and for good. The world may not see you, but I know that what you are made of is good. Sometimes you don't always show it. But, I know who I am working with. I know the imperfect nature of a human. And, I will stand beside you to see you for you, always. You don't always believe you are good. You don't always see good. But child, I always believe that you are good. I always see good in you. Grow that good seed. However tiny it may be. Come to Me for the rain, the shelter, and the sunshine. I promise you will grow to see good in you and in everything. Just as I see you.

Lord Jesus, thank You for always seeing good in me whether it be the tiniest seed or a seed growing rapidly. When You see good in me, what You see is a heart after You. That is the good You find precious, rare, and beautiful. It's not what I do, how I do it, or even how I look doing it. It's the private discipline to know You more each and every day. It's the "Jesus, Jesus, Jesus" cry at 4:30pm on a Tuesday afternoon because I need to muster up the strength to keep a toddler busy while making supper and decompressing from work. It's the gratitude cry on a Saturday morning walk. It's the 2:30am cry when a ridiculous thought of anxiety is determined to rob my sleep. It's the praise cry as my baby achieves a milestone. It's the mundane cry of health and protection over my family daily. It's the nervous cry as my husband and I lay side by side and talk about our future before we close our eyes. It's the excited cry as a long-awaited prayer has been answered. That's the good stuff. It's all of it. That's what You see. And that's what's good. When no one else does. Or no one else understands. Each cry out to You. No one will ever know my heart like You do, Lord. Thank You for seeing it and believing it is good.

Notes

Adi Welp

You Are Courageous

1 Samuel 17:34-37 – But David persisted. "I have been taking care of my father's sheep and goats," he said. "When a lion or a bear comes to steal a lamb from the flock, I go after it with a club and rescue the lamb from its mouth... I have done this to both lions and bears, and I'll do it to this pagan Philistine, too, for he has defied the armies of the living God! The Lord who rescued me from the claws of the lion and the bear will rescue me from this Philistine!"

My child, come to the silence to gain your courage. The private, quiet moments in your life matter the most. The world wants to tell you it's the loud parts of your life that are most worthy. The "look at me" or "it's my time to shine" mentality. They've got it all wrong. It is alone – just you and I – where I prepare you for what's to come. Be disciplined to meet with Me every day. Most days, it may feel like you're not getting anywhere with Me, but child, you are getting everywhere. One day you will see all the pieces fall and all the chips land… into place. Into the exact place I motioned for them all along. But that's not for your eyes right now. Your eyes are on Me. Trusting, obeying, starting with Me. Day in and day out. That is My only request. In our mundane meetings are where I build a character in you that the world cannot touch. A character that will make heads turn and people wonder what it is you have that they don't. I turned heads with My servant, David, and I will do it again, and again, and again. A teenage, shepherd boy. The youngest of his brothers and no comparison in strength or size. But the character of his heart, My child. It was no match. He did well with what I gave him in the quiet – protecting his sheep. So when I gave him Goliath with an audience, he was no different. Trust, obey, and start the fight with Me.

Lord Jesus, thank You for the story of David. Wow. His discipline, humbleness, faith, and courage. They all seem out of reach. But they're not, Lord. David demonstrates what great power comes from doing the small things well. When it was just he and his sheep, he fought off lions and bears to protect them. Nobody saw. Nobody gloated over him. He didn't share these victories with the world. No, he went to Jesus. He started with Jesus. And his heart was set on obeying and trusting that whatever animal came his way, he would not be shaken. So when Goliath stood before him, he was unamused. The Lord of Armies stood with him before and would again. Lord Jesus, may I do the small things well so that when I'm faced with the big things in life, good or bad, I would react unamused, like David – "Do you know my God?". Give me the courage to step away from the world and into my Father's presence. I don't need to see where all my pieces fall now, but I do need to see You, Jesus.

Notes

_____

_____

_____

_____

_____

_____

_____

_____

_____

_____

_____

_____

Adi Welp

You Are Human

Isaiah 55:9 – For just as the heavens are higher than the earth, so my ways are higher than your ways and my thoughts higher than your thoughts.

My child, time for an honest look into your heart. I am constantly working on you because I won't leave you as you were born. You are good. So good. But, you are also broken. You mess up. You were born with a selfish heart. I am sorry that's the way it is, My child. But let's look at it from a different angle. If you were perfect, where would My need be? When would I get the opportunity to love you? To give you grace? To watch you transform into the beautiful human I have intended you to be. Look at you recognizing a need for Me. Oh, you make My heart soar. I am all knowing, all powerful, and all good. I am perfect. You are not. But child, your imperfections don't define you. They don't hold you back or knock you down. No. Your imperfections strengthen you to look beyond yourself and to Me. When you look to Me, all the striving, pursuing, and desiring is put to an end. You become the person you truly wanted all along. And not from your own selfish desires but from an overflow of love that you pour into a relationship with Me. The overflow of our relationship touches the hearts of the people around you simply by putting in the effort with Me, not with them. My child, rest in your imperfections. I fill in the cracks of the vase so that the vase endlessly overflows with My goodness.

Lord Jesus, thank You for giving me a gut check today. Lately, my selfish thoughts have gotten in the way of my mission for You. I found myself wanting to be the best wife, mama, daughter, sister, friend, coworker, etc. because I wanted to look good… not because I wanted You to look good. Gulp. Thank You for Your boundless grace that washes over me. Lord, I need Your grace and renewal so often. Renew my mind so that all I see is You. Renew my thoughts so that the entirety of my focus is on Your will. Renew my heart so that my intentions come from a place of purity. Lord Jesus, I know I am human. I mess up more than I'd like to admit. Thank You for reminding me of Your sovereignty over my life. Please take the pressure of perfectionism off of me today. As it creeps into my thoughts, Lord, help me to recognize it right away and turn from it. Lord, I am human, but each day I pray my ways can be more aligned with Your ways and my thoughts more in tune with Your thoughts. Fill in all my cracks so that my vase can stand strong and overflow for You.

Notes

Adi Welp

You Are An Overcomer

1 Samuel 30:4-6 – …they wept until they could weep no more. David's two wives, Ahinoam from Jezreel and Abigail, the widow of Nabal from Carmel, were among those captured… But David found strength in the Lord his God.

You are defined by what I see, not what you see, My child. Read that again. You are defined by how I see you. You may see defeat and tears. You may see exhaustion that has left you on your knees. You may see a lost cause. "It's not worth it. I've tried that before. I'm not doing it again." You may see hopelessness and weakness. Beat down and hurt. You may see anxiousness and fear. "What am I doing with my life?" My precious son David felt all of this when the people he loved were taken from him. Weeping loudly, all he saw inside of him was despair and heartache. He saw an unbeatable circumstance. I saw a moveable mountain. He saw sadness. I saw hope. He saw a hurt soul. I saw a child in desperate need of his Father. But then, he looked up… he saw Me… and became an overcomer. Find your strength in Me today. You will press on. You will move that mountain a little more with each new day. You will overcome.

Lord Jesus, thank You for seeing what I cannot see. Sometimes my vision is blurred. I cannot see past what I think others are seeing… that I am silly, sensitive, overbearing, unprepared, nervous, not good enough, not worthy enough, and ultimately unwanted. But, God. Two words. But, God. You see me the opposite. You see a wisdom that is beyond the world's knowledge. You see a kindness that is underappreciated. You see a compassion that has just not yet been accepted. You see a confidence waiting to be unleashed. You see a child holding onto hope. You see a daughter. A mama. A wife. A sister. A friend. A coworker. A step-mom. A niece. A step-daughter. For who she really is. An overcomer. Thank You for not sitting back and letting the world define me. Thank You for reaching out Your hands to welcome me into the presence of what You see. Lord, may I have eyes today that see myself and others the way You see us. My strength, kindness, love, joy, peace, goodness, and radiance is found in You and in You alone.

Notes

Adi Welp

You Are Light

Psalm 46:10 – Be still, and know that I am God! I will be honored by every nation. I will be honored throughout the world.

Lay down your striving, My child. Lay it down. It no longer has a grip on you. You aren't getting to the outcome faster. Watching you is exhausting. I see you pushing for more. More advances in your career. More stuff so you can keep up with the trends. More pressure to be an all-star parent. More time to finish your to-do list at the end of each day. More family fun ideas to exhaust every minute of the weekend. More money to be able to do everything you want without crunching numbers. More, more, more. But when will it stop? When will you lay down the fight and run to Me? My arms are wide open. My path is known. My baggage is light. Take the pressure off. It doesn't belong to you. It never did. I didn't create you so that you would be burdened by worldly pressures. No, I created you to show others how to live differently in the midst of worldly pressures. Yes, the burdens are present. All around you. But it's how you meet the burdens head on and give them to Me. That's what's different, My child. The more, more, more – it doesn't own you. It doesn't drag you into the ground. It lifts you up to Me. It raises your hands and changes you. You are different, child – not because you don't strive. Because you strive for a "who" instead of a "what."

Lord Jesus, thank You for creating me to strive differently. To focus on You instead of the "whats" of the world. I don't always get it right. And, I frequently don't recognize it. I go through life often without realizing what it is that I'm trying to gain. Typically, it's not You. Typically, it's my own desires and wants. If I could just have this. If I could just get there. All for what? You're right, Lord Jesus. What am I going to do once I have that and get there? I'm going to look around and be standing in the same place I was. It's not until I just get more of You. Until I just hear Your voice repeatedly. Until I just see Your presence in the mundane. Until I just feel Your love lift me off my feet and set me back down, unburdened. Light. Oh so light, my Jesus. Pressure's off. How good that feels. Lord, help me to walk each day differently. Help me to put my effort into striving for someone instead of something. It's a different stride than the rest of the world. It may be slower. It may even be rejected by most. But it's safer. And it's a whole lot lighter.

Notes

Adi Welp

You Are Covered

2 Samuel 22:31 – God's way is perfect. All the Lord's promises prove true. He is a shield for all who look to him for protection.

Covered. Covered, My child. Think of a warm blanket on a cool night. Think of an umbrella on a rainy day. Think of a band aid on a fresh wound. I am all of those things for you. Comfort, security, and protection. Therefore, wherever you walk. Whatever lies ahead of you. Whatever is left behind. I am there. I was there. Just as I place the stars each night, I placed you here. It is not accidental. It is not by chance. You were handpicked for this moment. Do not fear. Do not shy away. Do not doubt. Walk along the path that could only be created by Me, and take refuge under My cover. You may feel the heat at times. Stand under My shade. You may be desperate for a drink. Fill your cup from My living word. You may experience an unexpected wild animal. Find that confident lion inside of you, and let her roar. You may lose a shoe. Learn that you grow the most in the uncomfortable. You make it to your destination. Look back and see that every moment was calculated, and in every moment, you were covered. My way is perfect. Trust the process.

Lord Jesus, thank You for covering me. Thank You for putting Your shield around me so that many times, all I see is one step in front of me. I laugh because I don't like it. I want to calculate my life and what's going to happen. But, I know You are intentional, Jesus. You don't show me the ending, 5 years from now, or even 5 hours from this moment. Because You don't want my fleeting emotions. You want my heart. You want my mind. You want my gaze to be on You. You want my obedience. My sureness in each step. I am picturing a tightrope, Lord. If I look down and only see a foot of the rope that is the perfect size for me to place my step, I do not fear. You show me one foot at a time of the rope, and I walk along in confidence knowing that's where my foot goes each time. If I look down to a wider vision and see 25 feet of rope ahead of me, I panic. Anxiety sets in. I either shut down and turn around or I am fearful the whole way. Thank You, Lord, for not showing me the ending. It was never mine to see. I see You. Covering me. Shielding me. I walk on.

You Are: A Journal of His Voice

Notes

Adi Welp

You Are Known

1 Kings 8:38-39 – "...and if your people Israel pray about their troubles, raising their hands toward this Temple, then hear from heaven where you live, and forgive. Give your people what their actions deserve, for you alone know each human heart."

How much do I know you? Much more than you know you. And even more than that. How much do I hear you? As much as every unsaid thought from you. And even more than that. How much do I give you? As much as the sand stretched before you. And even more than that. How much do you know Me? Do you long to find Me? And sit in My embrace. How much do you hear Me? Do you long to listen? And open up your heart. How much do you give Me? Do you long to surrender? And let My will be done. Child, every prayer you pray, every word unspoken, every thought imagined is Mine. It's Mine. I put it there. I know what you are going to pray, want to say, and think about because I know you. All of you. Fully known. There is no other person that could know you like I do. Hear you like I do. Love you like I do. I long for all of you, child. And even more than that.

Lord Jesus, thank You for seeing all of me. All of my human heart and still choosing me. Choosing to stay. Choosing to be. Choosing to know… me. All of me. Lord, it amazes me how well You know each heart. You don't miss a detail. You don't hold back. You jump into what makes my heart tick, and You do just that. You keep it ticking. You keep learning about me, hearing me, giving to me. Lord, You are a good, good Father. I am a mess. You know that. It's no surprise. I'm undone. Unpolished. Unwell. Yet, You say to me, "Child. Yes, you. Broken one. I know you. I know who I created you to be. You may be broken now, but you won't be broken forever. You can't fathom the things I've called you to. You are an unimaginable force to be reckoned with. You are grace, gentleness, and love, all sewn together with the strong will of a 2-year-old." Lord Jesus, today I hear Your voice. I know that call. I want to know it deeper, stronger. Jesus, help me to see You fully known as You see me.

Notes

Adi Welp

You Are Imperfectly Perfect

Psalm 73:23 – Yet I still belong to you; you hold my right hand.

My child, bring it in. I'm here to tell you a story. A story about a child so loved, so wanted, so dreamed of, and so held. It doesn't always feel like that, does it? Held. "What do you mean I'm held, Jesus? I feel alone, unheard, unseen. Going through the motions of life and wondering what am I missing in all of this?" My child, there will be seasons of assuredness. Of confidence. Of security. But as you know, there will also be seasons of doubt. Of confusion. Of distance. I am not distant. I may be testing… but not distant. It is easy to praise Me on the mountain. When all the stars are aligned and shining bright. It is difficult to see Me in the mundane. The unremarkable. When all the stars are present but you just can't seem to make out the Big Dipper. Child, I know you feel that. You are walking around life trying your best. Pouring into others. Waking up early for your daily bible discipline. Whispering prayers in the car, the office, and your son's bedroom when all's quiet. But why does it feel like something's missing? Why does it feel like you can't see Me in the everyday routine? Why do you feel like you're trying so hard to see and talk to a God who is not giving anything in return? Maybe that's just it, child. Maybe you're trying but trying alone. Trying, striving, forcing. Listen, child. Listen. I told you I wanted to tell you a story. Turn off your thoughts. Turn off your ambition. Turn off your pride. Let Me hold you. Listen to the beautiful story unfold.

Lord Jesus, thank You for speaking to me. Thank You for giving me an answer to a question that I've been grappling with for some time. My answer isn't "more." More good deeds. More bible verses read. More talking. It's actually "less." Less striving. Less pressure. Less of my voice. You speak to me best when I sit. At the computer, You and I converse. I come with questions. Confusion. Doubt. I leave with answers. Assuredness. Confidence. I think You don't speak to me, but You do. You are guiding my heart to hear Your voice as I type. The quiet, small voice inside. You are not distant from me like I once thought. You don't move. I do. I create the distance between us with my "more, more, more." You're just as close as ever. Inviting me back to the space where I hear You, and You hear me. You always have a story to tell. For You are the greatest storyteller, and You are the greatest story. Help me to never miss a moment listening to Your voice speaking to me as You hold me close.

Notes

_____

_____

_____

_____

_____

_____

_____

_____

_____

_____

_____

_____

_____

_____

_____

Adi Welp

You Are Worthy

Colossians 1:9-10 – ...We ask God to give you complete knowledge of his will and to give you spiritual wisdom and understanding. Then the way you live will always honor and please the Lord, and your lives will produce every kind of good fruit. All the while, you will grow as you learn to know God better and better.

Worthy. That's you. That's her. Worthy of a relationship with Me. That's the power of grace. And the power of Me, My child. That I would come down to call you worthy. No matter your upbringing, your social status, your college attended or career path pursued, your possessions, your present, or your future. You are worthy in this exact place due to one thing and one thing alone. You are My child. Not any child. I call you daughter. You call Me Father. See that young child raised by a single mom working all day and night to pay the bills. She calls Me Father. See that woman working in a high rise in the big city wishing for a husband someday. She calls Me Father. See that tired teacher. That lonely widow. That adopted child. That new mama. That drug addict. That entrepreneur. That spoiled daughter. They call Me Father. "Father! Father! Are You there?"
"Yes, child? What? What do you want? What do you need?"

Lord Jesus, thank You for responding to Your name. Like a tired mother answering her child for the 100th time that day, "What, child?" Yet, I don't think You tire, Lord. You don't tire of giving me the answer I want and need. Even when I seek and ask and doubt You 100 times a day. And You certainly extend me patience and grace as I try to figure out what I mean to You. What I mean in this world. Isn't every one of Your children seeking the same thing? Love. To be called enough. To be praised. To be worthy. To be told well done. To be comforted. To be secure. To be fully heard, known, and seen. To be in her Father's presence. That's the true seeking. Not for a different job, a solution, a new pair of shoes, a new husband, a cure, a greener patch of grass. For a person. For a person – that goes by Dad.

Notes

Adi Welp

You Are Settled

Deuteronomy 32:2 – Let my teaching fall on you like rain; let my speech settle like dew. Let my words fall like rain on tender grass, like gentle showers on young plants.

This has been a tough pill to swallow, hasn't it, My child? Settled. "You mean slow down, God? You mean don't try to do it all?" What you're learning is that settling in Me is dependence. Complete surrender to My embrace. The opportunity for Me to scoop you up and not leave you. Not forsake you. Not let you figure it out on your own or walk away with a half-hearted, "Good luck with that." No, child. Not at all. You're learning that settling in Me is complete peace. It's "Lord, I need You. I'm confused. I didn't think it would be this way. What am I supposed to do? Where am I supposed to go? I'm scared. I'm worried. There's a lot on my plate. How am I supposed to do it all? I just need You." Child, I am here. Right here. In your presence as you think. Soak in My grace, and let it settle like dew over your life. A gentle rain on new grass. When My rain settles on you, child, you are changed. A shower on tender plants. When you are weak, child, you are at your strongest. Just as the grass grows after a fresh rain has settled on it, child, look at you thrive as you settle in Me. With you, I am well pleased.

Lord Jesus, thank You for Your grace. That I am able to come into Your presence, day after day, dropping off my weaknesses in exchange for loads of Your grace. Lord, I have found myself more than ever at Your doorstep. Knocking? More like stumbling into Your presence. Maybe it's since becoming a mama, Lord. Since being in control of things is just no longer possible. It never was. But it was easier to mask when I was just in charge of myself. Now that another life has come into my care, there's no masking. There's no pretending I can do it all myself. I am quickly realizing that. Settling in You is not only the sole option, it's the best option. It's the sweetest treasure. There is no one I'd rather hand over control to than You, Father. Take my life and my child's, and do what You will. For Your outcomes are good. They are greater than we could ever imagine. Saying that truth out loud frees me from fear, worry, or guilt. I am light – as light as the dew on the grass after a fresh fallen rain.

Notes

Adi Welp

You Are Desired

Isaiah 60:19 – No longer will you need the sun to shine by day, nor the moon to give its light by night, for the Lord your God will be your everlasting light, and your God will be your glory.

My child, I desire you. To desire is to wish for something to happen. I don't desire anything more than a relationship with you. Your heart. Your mind. Your actions. I desire to talk with you. Like old friends. I desire to give to you. More than the moon and stars. You want the moon and stars in this life. Don't you, child? But listen. The moon and stars light up the night. What happens when morning comes? They fade. The things you think are the "moon and stars" fade. They do not sustain, last, or keep. Desire Me, child, and you get more than the moon and stars. You get a Son that does not dim. Everlasting, eternal, infinite. Don't those words sound secure? Safe. Needed. It is what you need. I would know – I made you. My only desire for you to have in this life is Me. Sounds simple, not? Just Me. Desire Me. Watch your troubles go away. Desire Me. Watch your fear subside. Desire Me. Watch your guilt vanish. Desire Me. Watch your worry waiver. Desire Me. Watch blessings on blessings on blessings unfold. My child, I will always desire you, but will you desire Me?

Lord Jesus, thank You for desiring me. Thank You for wanting me and the best for me. Jesus, I had an epiphany the other day, thinking of my own child. I saw some areas of struggle, and I wept. I wanted to prevent any hardship. I wanted future struggles to be nonexistent for him. I wanted to take away any future pain. I wanted to give him the moon and stars. And more. Then I came to the realization. When I thought about giving him the moon and stars, I thought about giving him a hardship free life. But wait. What if giving him the moon and stars is different? What if giving him the moon and stars is giving him Jesus? You. Showing him how to talk to You, cry to You, come to You. Isn't that the moon and stars? Isn't that what life is all about? That's better than the moon and stars. I cannot take away any future pain or struggles, but I can lead him to the One who can. Jesus, help me to desire You and be an example of a life filled with the moon and stars.

You Are: A Journal of His Voice

Notes

You Are Still

Isaiah 26:3 – You will keep in perfect peace all who trust in you, all whose thoughts are fixed on you!

Still. I think you need to look up the definition, My child. I say that in a playful but honest way. This world doesn't know much about stillness. You have already done or made a list to do hundreds of little things today. That's just the thing though, child. Little things. Miniscule. In the grand plan of your life, most things on your to-do list are little. Now I'm not saying to neglect the responsibilities I've given you. No, child. Never. But, I am saying to put Me before them. Be still with Me for a moment to breathe in the big things I am planning for you. Watch Me turn your little things into big things just by being with Me. Be still with Me as much as you breathe. A lofty goal? Yes. But, I'm just asking you to try. I'm calling you to various moments of stillness each and every day. Deep breaths before a big meeting. Two minutes to sip coffee in your quiet, dark house. Birds chirping on an afternoon walk. Your baby napping. Looking out your window as you do the daily dishes. Drives to work. A few seconds before you help your next patient, student, or customer. Doesn't seem as lofty now does it, child? Remember Me. I will never forget to call you.

Lord Jesus, thank You for slowing me down today. What started as chores, taking care of the baby, yard work, and a running to-do list in my head has stilled for a moment. The baby is sleeping, the bulk of the mess is picked up, and the urge to take a nap or binge Netflix is calling. But Lord, I know what I need is You. Your cry for me is louder. You slow me down to remind me who I am. I am loved, secure, cared for, and adored. I am filled with peace in this moment. Pure peace. My heart is calm. I know this moment won't last long externally. The baby will awake. The sink will refill with dishes. The outside world will carry on with events, duties, hardships, and joys. But internally, Lord, keep me in Your peace. Internally, remind me of this moment over and over and over again. So that my heart is in a state of peace wherever I go. So that my heart is with You, always. As often as I breathe, Lord, call me to Your stillness and help me to answer with "Yes, Father. I am coming."

You Are: A Journal of His Voice

Notes

Adi Welp

You Are Relieved

Philippians 4:7 – Then you will experience God's peace, which exceeds anything we can understand. His peace will guard your hearts and minds as you live in Christ Jesus.

Welcome back, My child. I know it's been a hard few days, weeks, months for you. I've seen. I've heard. I haven't missed a thing. All I care about is that you're back. Like a child finds his way back to his mama in an unknown environment. You were in the unknown. I saw you. Your mind tossed and turned. You had moments back in My peace. Then you got swept away again. Why does it keep happening? You wanted to make it stop. You wanted to come back to Me. To accept My peace. My joy. My love. It's hard, child, until you know who I am. But now, O Jacob, listen to the Lord who created you. O Israel, the one who formed you says, "Do not be afraid, for I have ransomed you. I have called you by name; you are mine." Mine. Without Me, you don't have a heartbeat. You don't have a husband, a job, a child, a house, a this, or a that. You fill in the blank. You are Mine. Stop trying to do life without Me. Stop sitting in the unknown, worrying about tomorrow. I am known. Know that I am all powerful. Know that I am all knowing. Know that I am ever present. Know that I am the answer. The answer you've been searching for in the unknown. Know it's Me. Now stay here. In the known with Me. And live.

Lord Jesus, thank You for this day. Thank You for this opportunity to be ever present in today and in what is known – that You are present here today. Lord, help me to soak in what it means to be back in Your presence. It's safe. It's peace. It's joy. It's relief. Help me to immerse myself in what is known every day. Distractions, lies, thoughts, deceit, fear, worry, etc. won't stop. I know this. But armor me with the truth every single day. Armor me with what it means to be filled with Your spirit. Guide me back to Your loving presence when I go astray. When my thoughts overcome me and I feel doubt, take me back to who I am and who You are. Help me to live differently from those around me. Help me to be so filled with Your peace – a peace I cannot comprehend – that when worries arise, I go to the One who holds me. I pray, and I leave it with You. I don't take it out of the room. I leave it in Your hands. Lord, discipline me to keep coming back. That child who comes back to his mama. He is unsettled until he is in her presence. He is scared, worried, and troubled. As soon as his eyes meet his mama's, he melts. The weight of his body lightens because his whole world is in view. Yes, Jesus. That's You. My vision isn't always clear, but help me come back to who I know You to be – my whole world.

Notes

Adi Welp

You Are Made For Gratitude

Psalm 9:1 – I will praise you, Lord, with all my heart; I will tell of all the marvelous things you have done.

What takes you back to gratitude, child? What stirs your heart to sing My praises? Is it nature? A friend? A book? A drowsy rest on the couch? A car ride? A concert? Whatever it is, go there. And go there often. Every breath, a word of thanks. Every move, an expression of praise. Every second, "Thank You, Jesus. Thank You for this day." A day that has been written long before you entered into the world. I just breathed it into existence today, but the thought of this day was created a long time ago. When you walk through this day remember your blessings. But also… remember the One who blesses. Give thanks not only on mountaintops but also in the valleys because the One that blesses occupies the valleys more than the mountaintops. Give thanksgiving for a God who knows when you need a mountaintop and a valley. Bloom, My child. In whatever landscape you find yourself in. You don't ever have to wonder or question My intentions. They are good. They are to bless. They are to give thanks. Give thanks for this moment. Right now. What a beautiful flower I see budding.

Lord Jesus, thank You for giving me a heart of thanks. Right now, gratitude is found looking out my bedroom window. Various bees and butterflies of different sizes come to gently land on a bush that has not bloomed all summer. Yet, in the middle of October, it's in full bloom, bright and beautiful. These insects – they're taken care of. All year round, they don't question where their food will come from. You designed the plants to perfectly bloom at different seasons in order for them to always be taken care of. Always. How grateful they must be to find a large plant in bloom for them in every season. But, if You take care of the butterflies and the bees, how much more do You take care of me? How much more did You perfectly create my story? A story of blooming in different seasons. Although some seasons it's hard to see the growth, it's always there. Although some seasons it's difficult to raise my hands in gratitude, there's always something to lift up my voice in praise. How beautiful would life be if we, like the butterflies, thank You in every season for putting in front of us the exact thing we need. What a beautiful view of life that would be. A lens that never dulls, scratches, or muddies. Help me, Jesus, to see the world with a lens of gratitude in every season of blooming.

Notes

_____

_____

_____

_____

_____

_____

_____

_____

_____

_____

_____

_____

_____

_____

_____

_____

_____

_____

Adi Welp

You Are Given Grace

John 1:16 – From his abundance we have all received one gracious blessing after another.

Fullness. Defined as the state of being filled to capacity. Yes, child. Soak that in. Lacking nothing. Receive grace upon grace from My fullness. I do not lack. When I pour My grace on you, you don't lack. I see you chasing after that nonexistent marker. Like a dog chasing after his own tail. He won't ever catch it. Just like you won't ever be in a state of complete fullness without My grace. I see you go into the day, child. You are eager, your eyes full of desire. You completed your prayer time, you got the baby off to the sitter, and you peacefully awaited who you would come into contact with today. But as the day unfolds, nothing is happening like you imagined. There's hurt, worry, selfishness, confusion, etc. "But Lord, I prayed for peace from my anxiety, so why did I doubt and run to Google?" "But Lord, I prayed for Your words to flow through me, so why was that conversation awkward?" Defeated. You end the day with so many moments of gratitude and joy, but what moments keep replaying through your mind? The moments that you weren't so called "perfect." The moments you showed need for Me. Need for My grace. Child, I'm not saying do not strive to be a better version of yourself. But child, strive more at aligning your heart with Me. Align your heart with being less concerned about perfectionism and more concerned with the act of grace. Through every situation, in every moment, at any second, receive Me – the author and perfecter of grace. I promise, you will lack nothing.

Lord Jesus, thank You for speaking to me about Your grace lately. When You repeat, I listen. Lately, the words feel like a tackle on a football field. I am knocked down by the truth of needing You and Your grace. And I am altogether wondering why can't I get this right? You are my source of fullness through Your grace, so why do my days sometimes feel like an endless pursuit of something I will never obtain? Lord Jesus, align my heart with Your fullness. Help me to strive for perfect peace in You instead of peace in a "perfect" life. I am beginning to realize the perfect life comes from a relationship with You. Fill my heart so full that I realize I lack nothing in You.

Fill my heart so full that grace washes over the parts that feel guilt. Fill my heart so full that whatever I am "searching" for cannot be seen apart from You. In You, I receive grace upon grace. And I receive fullness that doesn't know defeat.

Notes

Adi Welp

You Are Made With Him In Mind

Song of Songs 4:7 – You are altogether beautiful, my darling, beautiful in every way.

My child, you are altogether beautiful. You are alive. A spirit that shines and cannot be dulled. You are magic. Eyes that twinkle with wonder. Giggles that go on for a long time. You are rich. Rich in kindness, beauty, gentleness, patience, and love. Everything I made you to be. You are nothing less. You are made with a God-filled heart. It bursts when you truly tap into who you are. Your mission is clear. Your eyes are set. Your mind is focused. You know exactly who you are when you tap into who I made you to be. You push aside comparison, jealousy, anger, and doubt. You step into grace. Freedom to be exactly who I made you to be. Don't be scared, My child, you weren't made like the rest of them. You weren't made with the same abilities or weaknesses. No need to compare. It will never make sense. No, you were made you. I look down and smile. My beautiful, faithful child. Don't we all look at our children that way when they truly tap into who we know them to be? Live in that today, child. See yourself the way your Father sees His child.

Lord Jesus, thank You for reminding me of who I am. These words give life to my soul and a fire in my heart. If only we all could tap into who You have called us to be. Lord, make it my mission to help others see themselves the way You see them. Altogether beautiful. No flaw in them. Place a fire in my soul to bring out the best in others. The things You see. The things that are hard to recognize in ourselves. Sometimes I am so busy worrying about me, Lord, but I want to worry about You. I want to worry about not becoming who You made me to be. You whisper, "Remain on the vine, (name). You won't falter. You will be exactly who I want you to be." No difficult hoops to jump through. Simply, seeking You with everything I have for the rest of my life. Help me, Jesus. Simply said but a hard task in today's world. Lord, help me to not miss a beat. Help me to see You in each step I take. Help me to be so lost in You and others that I lose myself. I was made with You in mind, not me. Help me to be Your version of altogether beautiful, not the world's.

You Are: A Journal of His Voice

Notes

Adi Welp

You Are Sweet

Proverbs 24:13-14 – My child, eat honey, for it is good, and the honeycomb is sweet to the taste. In the same way, wisdom is sweet to your soul. If you find it, you will have a bright future, and your hopes will not be cut short.

My child, I have made you with sweetness in mind. Sweet as honey. Oh, so sweet. Honey is not only sweet but healing. Designed to make you well again. Whole. Seek honey when you are sick but also for wisdom. Wisdom heals your weary bones, strengthens your anxious mind, and finds your wandering heart. You don't have to wander any longer. Wisdom is right in front of you. Find it, and you have found a treasure. Find it, and you have a future. Find it, and you have everlasting hope. See how sweet wisdom is? Like tasting a honeysuckle picked straight from the bush as a kid. A shot of sweetness to your body. What started as a curious act led to pure goodness. Child, My wisdom is the same for you. I see you are curious. Curious how to live a life full of hope and trust in My plan. Take a shot of My wisdom and never be the same. You will have a treasure hidden in the field. You will have a future written by Me. Find Me today, and let Me whisper to you all that I want you to know.

Lord Jesus, thank You for teaching me about Your wisdom. I often don't realize my wisdom and Your wisdom are two totally different things. My wisdom is finite and variable. While Yours is infinite and steady. I think I am wise. I think I know what I need. Lord, am I wrong. In every situation I face, help me to look in the mirror at what You are speaking to me. Help me to seek Your wise counsel and push my selfish desires to the side. Nine times out of ten my "wisdom" is my inner voice trying to make me believe that it is You speaking to me. Nine times out of ten I need Your wisdom to show me what I am lacking in myself. I need the work, not my situation. Lord, I'm willing to put in the work if what I find is You. If what I find is a treasure, everlasting hope, and a future, Lord, I am in. Help me to drink up Your wisdom today. May Your sweet, sweet wisdom flow through my bones and leave me with a thirst for more of You. Just like there's nothing sweeter than honey, there's nothing more powerful in my life than Your wisdom.

Notes

Adi Welp

You Are Not Forgotten

Hebrews 12:1-2 – ...And let us run with endurance the race God has set before us. We do this by keeping our eyes on Jesus, the champion who initiates and perfects our faith.

Here you sit. You wonder. You find yourself in a period of waiting, My child. Waiting is hard. Waiting exercises patience, discipline, and strength. Waiting on Me to move does not mean forgotten. In your waiting, I am working. Working tirelessly to knit everything together perfectly for your story. You don't see that. Sometimes you don't believe that. It's okay, child. I won't give up on your human mind that cannot comprehend all that I am and all that I do. Don't give up on Me in the waiting. Run the race set before you with eyes lifted to your Maker. For I am the only constant in your world. The only truth. And the only answer. Forget worldly advice, the trends that fade from one season to the next. Forget Google, the answers that are based on opinion and not on truth. Forget your own voice, when not aligned with Mine, it leads you astray. But don't forget Me. My child, don't ever forget Me. I haven't forgotten you.

Lord Jesus, thank You for never forgetting me as Your child. Sometimes, I forget just who my Father is. Just how all knowing, all loving, and all powerful He is. Forgetting the world seems next to impossible in a room full of distractions. Lord, help me to not become so obsessed with the world's opinions that I lose my purpose. My purpose to be Your child. To be loved by You and to love You. How beautiful that is. How simple that sounds. Lord Jesus, give me the strength and discipline to walk in this faith. Help me to never forget You in a painted sky. Never forget You in the eyes of my child gazing up at me. Never forget You in the heartache of a tragedy… in the smile of a stranger… in the worry of the unforeseeable future… in the beauty of a simple life. You are always there. You've never left. You've never forgotten me.

Notes

You Are His

Matthew 6:33 – Seek the Kingdom of God above all else, and live righteously, and he will give you everything you need.

Welcome, My most precious one. I'm so happy you are here. Coming into this space and moment with Me is the most important choice you have made all day. Makes those decisions looming about work, your family, your relationships, your future, etc. a little less significant, right? You have made a choice to live in the light of your Father right now, and oh, I have so much to pour into you. What a delight you are to Me. Yes, you. Wherever you are. In your joy or sorrow, peace or anxiety, love or anger. You have noticed Me. And child, at that, I smile. I not only smile, I beam. A beam so bright it cannot be contained. You think you can contain it inside of your human body, but you cannot. It is a "watermark" used on all of My children. A watermark is defined as "visible when held against the light and typically identifies the maker." Woah. This beam I am talking about in you is made visible only in My presence and identifies who I am to all the world. Do some lights shine brighter? Sure. That's up to you, My child. You've made one stride forward with Me today, now come back tomorrow for another… and another… and another. I promise this story will be worthwhile.

Lord Jesus, thank You for Your light. A light that is so beautiful, powerful, yet simple and quiet. That afternoon light streaming onto the lace tablecloth spread across the dining room table. Making for a peace-filled, glimmer of hope. Making me smile at the simplest beauty. A new week welcomes me, Lord. Give me the heart of my child this week – full of joy, hope, and light. It beams across his face as he takes in the simplest of moments. What a gift he has. What a gift You offer. Lord, my eyes, ears, mind, and heart are open. I am ready to seek You and Your light. Help me not to miss moments to brighten the beam inside of me. I am ready to seek You and Your light. Seeking You is the anthem I want in my days and the anthem I need. My strides ahead are uncertain but beautifully lit. They tell the story of You if I let them.

Notes

Adi Welp

You Are Understood

Proverbs 3:5-6 – Trust in the Lord with all your heart; do not depend on your own understanding. Seek his will in all you do, and he will show you which path to take.

Child, I understand all of you. Your human mind was not designed to understand everything happening around you, to you, in your past, present, or future. Your human mind was made to trust. To trust that I know you better than anyone. To trust that I will provide when you seek Me. To trust that your understanding alone is not enough. Do not trust your wavering mind. Trust in Me with everything you have. Like the game you played when you were younger – "trust fall." Eyes closed, arms crossed, fall back into My plans for you. You think you know, don't you, My child? That is why your mind wanders here and there. The wandering creates worry. The worry creates a definitive end to your situation. No, no, no, child. This is not the end. Know who I am and what I can do for you. Know that this situation in front of you is only merely understood by you and fully understood by Me. I see everything that happened before it, around it, and what is yet to come. Oh, child, give Me permission to speak into you what I know and understand about you in this moment.

Lord Jesus, thank You for Your reassurance. You assure me that You understand everything happening in my life, and it's all intentional – for Your purpose. That doesn't make the "trust fall" easy, Lord. Eyes blinking to catch a glimpse of the plan, arms shaking as they cross, leaning slightly back and then putting my leg down out of habit to make sure You'll catch me. Lord, help my trust in You to surpass any other trust I've given to someone or something in my life. A trust that seems beyond my own human ability. Help me to fall heavy back into Your arms. You are my Father, looking down on me and moving each piece and each path in my life until it aligns with Your plan. Like a parent directing a child who is learning to ride a bike. Slow down on that rocky road. Stay away from that muddy path. That hill is steep, but don't be afraid to try…. gentle nudges that are never directing but always leading. You understand. Speak to me about what I need to know now.

Notes

Adi Welp

You Are Chosen

Esther 4:14 – ...Who knows if perhaps you were made queen for just such a time as this?

Child, you feel Me nudging you. You've felt it for a while. But this, but that. But life got busy, but remaining near Me was hard… but, but, but, but… but God. I haven't stopped nudging your heart. I haven't stopped believing in you. You may have, but I haven't. Perhaps, I designed you to do this very thing. This very thing that frightens you to your core but also excites your weary heart. You were made to do a lot of things, My child. I give you many callings, but child, not all the callings hold the same weight. There are some that stir your soul like you've never felt. That's why it's scary, right? That's why you question it, right? It feels out of the ordinary, unlikely, and absurd. Child, wasn't I all those things? Out of the ordinary. Unlikely. Absurd. A king, born in a humble stable – that's not ordinary. A Savior in human form resurrected into Heaven – highly unlikely. A leader taking the form of a humble servant and going against all the ways of the world – how absurd. Seems like you and I have a lot in common, huh, My child? Choose to go where I am leading you, for My calling is never mistaken.

Lord Jesus, thank You for choosing me. A highly unlikely person. Perhaps Your very words laid on my heart today make me tear up because Your call is so obvious. Suddenly, Your plan doesn't feel unreachable. Lord, I ask that You cover this calling entirely in Your love, grace, and peace. I pray that You would lead each unstable step of mine. I pray that You would pour courage into each doubtful thought. I pray that You would seep Your wisdom into my veins. Perhaps I am chosen for this. Perhaps it's not out of the ordinary, unlikely, or absurd. Perhaps it's who You made me to be all along. What a beautiful thought to pursue one of the very things You had in mind for me as You formed me in my mother's womb. There is not another time. See that's the thing with time, Lord. It is finite and fleeting. It goes by way too fast. Help me to be careful to not miss this time You are giving me right now.

Notes

Adi Welp

You Are Different

Jeremiah 29:13 – If you look for me wholeheartedly, you will find me.

You are learning, My child. Little by little. I see the growth in your heart and in your home. You know I am the everlasting source of joy. Not fickle and fleeting matters. I am proud. Oh so proud of who you are becoming. Sing praise. Take heart. Be grateful. You are delightful and delighted in. This overwhelming feeling of peace. This search for Me. This growing bond. It's not over. Not until we meet face to face one day. I am teaching you how to take each day as it comes. I am teaching you not how to survive your earthly mission but how to thrive in it. How to be so completely wrapped up in My presence that it is hard not to gravitate towards you. Like a magnet, My child. The way you live in Me will attract but also push away some. Do not be discouraged. You are too strong of a daughter to be shaken by the ones who turn away. Love them hard. Love them anyway. You will catch them off guard and grow interest. "What's she have that's so different?" Me. Let's take on the world together.

Lord Jesus, thank You for calling me to higher things. Thank You for trusting me with Your plans. Thank You for not leaving my side as they are carried out. Lord, I am so overwhelmed with gratitude. That when I search for You. Whenever I come. Wherever I come. Whoever I come with. You answer. You are there. And, You are bright. An indescribable light carving my way. You teach me, show me, love me, and give me grace upon grace upon grace. Lord, thank You. I pray this friendship only gains momentum. I pray it only magnifies and illuminates. You are not only a good, good Father but a good, good friend. A friend that I have never met face to face but so fully trust because You have met me. You met me at the birth of my child. In the peace of an answered prayer. In the middle of my bedroom on my knees. In the exhaustion of a sick baby. In the midst of job changes, house changes, life changes. You have met me, and in those moments, I have never met anyone like You before. You are different and make me different. Let's go together.

You Are: A Journal of His Voice

Notes

Adi Welp

You Are Changed

Galatians 2:20 – My old self has been crucified with Christ. It is no longer I who live, but Christ lives in me. So I live in this earthly body by trusting in the Son of God, who loved me and gave himself for me.

Lose yourself, child. Tear off the desires you so desperately hold onto. It's okay to have desires, My child. For a joyful marriage, for a baby boy or girl, for a fulfilling career, for a house, for financial freedom, for a friend, for a loving community, etc. I want all those things for you. But when you start putting them above Me, they become unattainable. They are simply wishful thinking without Me. Want Me? Desire Me? Lose yourself to Me. All of you. Not just a quarter of that list – no, all of it. Hand it to Me, and start to pray. Form a relationship with Me. Then, watch all the pieces fall into place. Maybe some pieces of the puzzle look a little different than expected. Maybe some pieces have curves and dips that you weren't anticipating. But your story is the most beautiful puzzle I have ever created. Without Me, you get to the end of your road, and you're frustrated that you've lost a piece, or two, or three. With Me each piece fits together just as I designed it. When you start living for Me… for anyone but yourself, your life magnifies. Your purpose is clear. Peace is known. Love is perfected. Your life is found.

Lord Jesus, thank You for designing my puzzle and fitting all the pieces together as I surrender each part of my life. Lord, search me. Find the pieces of my heart that I still hold back from You. Help me to hand over those pieces. I know You are faithful. I know You are trustworthy. I know You are more than capable of taking those pieces. When it's hard to give them up, give me strength, courage, and an act of faith. Lord, I want more than anything for Your will to be my will. I want more than anything to complete the very things You have set apart for me. I want more than anything for Your heartbeat to be one with mine inside of me – that I no longer have a heartbeat because it's Yours. Magnify the peace, love, and joy in my heart as I lose myself to You. May the outpouring of my heart onto others be of no effort to me because it is not from me but from You. May You be the reason for everything I do.

Notes

we bring dreams to life™
advbookstore.com

www.ingramcontent.com/pod-product-compliance
Lightning Source LLC
Chambersburg PA
CBHW080608090426
42735CB00017B/3368